Logic, the truth-speaking huntress, with her questioning bow, syllogistic sword, and arm of argument, crushing entire species of fallacies underfoot. From the Margarita Philosophica, *by Gregor Reisch, Freiburg, 1503.*

Bloomsbury USA

An imprint of Bloomsbury Publishing Plc

1385 Broadway   50 Bedford Square
New York   London
NY 10018   WC1B 3DP
USA   UK

www.bloomsbury.com

BLOOMSBURY and the Diana logo are trademarks of
Bloomsbury Publishing Plc

First published 2016

ISBN: HB: 978-1-63286-445-1

Library of Congress Cataloging-in-Publication Data is available.

2 4 6 8 10 9 7 5 3 1

Designed and typeset by Wooden Books Ltd, Glastonbury, UK

Printed in the U.S.A. by Worzalla, Stevens Point, Wisconsin

To find out more about our authors and books visit
www.bloomsbury.com. Here you will find extracts, author interviews,
details of forthcoming events, and the option to sign up for our newsletters.

Bloomsbury books may be purchased for business or promotional use.
For information on bulk purchases please contact Macmillan Corporate and
Premium Sales Department at specialmarkets@macmillan.com.

LOGIC

THE ANCIENT ART OF REASON

Earl Fontainelle

BLOOMSBURY
NEW YORK · LONDON · OXFORD · NEW DELHI · SYDNEY

Dilectissimæ uxori suæ consecrat scriptor maximis cum gratiis hoc opusculum.

Thanks to the Warburg Institute for the use of their wonderful picture library. Image on p.vi from the M.C.Escher Company. Cartoons from Cartoonstock, except p.39 by Merrily Harpur. Further Reading: Aristotelian logic is well-presented in Sister Miriam Joseph's The Trivium: The Liberal Arts of Logic, Grammar, and Rhetoric *(Paul Dry Books 2002); for a good introduction to modern logic, try* The Logic Book *by Merrie Bergmann, James Moor & Jack Nelson (McGraw-Hill, 1990); to further your recognition of Fallacies, try* How to Win Every Argument, *by Madsen Pirie (Bloomsbury, 2006). To explore the wonderful world of Lewis Carol, read* The Annotated Alice, *edited by Martin Gardner (Norton & Co., 1999, Penguin).*

DIALETTICA

Above: Dialectic catches a slippery fish and a forked-tongued dragon in her fine logical net. From Somma di Tutte le Scienze, Aurelio Marinati, Rome, 1587

CONTENTS

Waterval by M.C. Escher (1961) is a beautiful visual representation of logical paradox (see p.42). All the individual elements of perspective make sense (the premises are true) and fit together on the page (the reasoning is valid), but the resulting image does not make sense (the conclusion is paradoxical).

INTRODUCTION

Everyone has had the experience of hearing a series of statements and thinking, 'That's logical'. Most of us seem innately to be able to reason from causes to effects. Every time we cross the road and avoid an oncoming car we are exercising our rational faculty. A small child, though, may be *unable* to make the connection between 'speeding car' and 'need-to-get-out-of-the-way'. So how do we get from the childhood state to one where we avoid the car as a matter of course? How do we create rules for *valid inference*?

While *reason* enables us to plan for the future, understand the past, and engage successfully with the present, *logic* is interested in the laws by which reason operates. Logicians want to know what makes one argument valid, and another plain wrong. This can be very useful, because people do not always think or speak the truth: they can be in error, lie, and 'rationalize' in crooked ways. For this reason, logic was considered the foundation of the three linguistic liberal arts (the *trivium* of logic, grammar, and rhetoric):

> *Of all the arts the first and most general is logic, then grammar, and last of all rhetoric, since there can be much use of reason without speech, but no use of speech without reason.* – John Milton, preface to The Art of Logic

This book explores the fundamental elements of practical logic and the process of reasoning in action. Along the way, the reader will be challenged to question everyday assumptions, to identify common logical fallacies, to wrestle with intractable paradoxes, and to take part in the ongoing search for truth.

DIALECTIC
and the Socratic method

We all have opinions. We all argue sometimes. In ancient Greece, when two or more philosophers used reasoned arguments to try to get to the truth of something over which they disagreed, they were said to be engaged in *dialectic* (from Gr. *dialegein*, to converse or dispute).

There are many ways to win an argument. The 5th-century BC Greek Sophists delighted in the arts of *oratory* (public speaking) and *debate* (oratorical competition), using *rhetoric* (clever linguistic devices) to persuade audiences and to demonstrate their own *aretē* (excellence). However, Socrates [470-399 BC] argued that *truth* mattered most, and that this could be best revealed through reason and logic in discussion.

To tease out the truth, Socrates employed a method which involved a number of steps:

1. Agatha asserts a THESIS: "Justice should treat everyone equally".

2. Socrates gets Agatha to agree to FURTHER PREMISES: "Surely you would agree that someone who is mad is not responsible for their actions?"

3. Socrates shows how these new premises imply the opposite of the original thesis: "So Justice should not treat everyone equally."

4. A NEW THESIS, more refined, is now advanced.

This technique was developed by Plato, Aristotle, and medieval and 19th century philosophers. Today it commonly takes the form:

1. THESIS: *I say! Don't you think ... Sheila is wonderful.*

2. ANTITHESIS: *On the contrary! I disagree ... She hurt Bill terribly.*

3. SYNTHESIS: *Let's try again! ... Yes, Sheila is complicated.*

While *dialectic* describes what people *do* every day as they dispute and reason back and forth, *logic* (from Gr. *logos*, 'reason' or 'speech') deals with the aspect of dialectic which is concerned with *validity*.

Over the centuries, the techniques by which the truth of statements and the validity of arguments have been determined and measured have changed immeasurably. Modern logical languages are so unforgiving that a single spelling mistake or wrong *Boolean operator* (*see page 48*) in a large computer program can bring a country to its knees.

These mathematical logical languages are not, however, the primary subject of this book. These pages instead mostly deal with the kind of logic we all use every day, the logic inherent in our spoken language, the logic that we use to convince children to brush their teeth, the logic we use to convince politicians to care for our future.

Some philosophers claim that true dialectic is a way of life resulting in a transcendent apprehension of truth. *The Seventh Platonic Epistle* sets the highest philosophic truth beyond the reach of words:

> *For it is not at all speakable like other subjects of study, but from much working together on the matter itself and living in company, suddenly a light, as it were leaping from fire, kindles in the soul, and (thenceforth) grows on its own.*

Pl. Ep. VII (341c4-d1)

Left: Woodcut of teacher and student, Strassburg, 1499. The medieval tradition continued the Classical practice of philosophical dialectic, with teachers and students disputing together over logical problems. In modern times, logic has evolved into something of a solitary art, but it only truly comes to life when people engage in dialectic.

3

TRUTH AND FALLACY
two wrongs don't make a right

In logical reasoning the goal is less understanding *that* something is true and more understanding (or explaining) *why* something is true. For thousands of years, philosophers have held that in an *argument*,

TWO THINGS ARE NECESSARY FOR A SOUND CONCLUSION:

   A. The premises must be true, and
   B. The reasoning must be valid.

Validity depends on the types of inference made in the argument (the *form* of the argument), and has nothing to say about the truth of the premises or the conclusion. So, in fact,

AN ARGUMENT MAY BE VALID WITHOUT BEING SOUND:

   1. PREMISE: *If the grass is green, it's Monday.* ✗
   2. PREMISE: *The grass is green.* ✓
   ∴ THEREFORE: *It is Monday.* ✗ but valid

This unsound but valid *modus ponens* argument (*see p. 20*) is nonsensical because the initial premise is false. And similarly:

AN INVALID ARGUMENT CAN HAVE A TRUE CONCLUSION:

   1. *All flowers are plants.* ✓   2. *Roses are plants;* ✓
   ∴ *Roses are flowers.* ✓ but invalid

This argument is invalid because its middle

All cats have four legs.
I have four legs.
Therefore, I am a cat.

4

term is undistributed (*see p. 15*). Invalid reasoning causes flawed arguments, which are known as *fallacies*. There are two main species of these sublogical creatures:

1. **FORMAL FALLACIES** are problems with the form of the argument. They involve invalid inferences, so are said to be formally invalid. One nasty formal fallacy is the CONCLUSION WHICH DENIES PREMISES.

   "No-one goes to that bar any more!" "Why?" "It's too crowded!" – Yogi Berra

2. **INFORMAL FALLACIES** arise from the matter rather than the form of the argument. Linguistic ambiguity, sneaky misdirection, and other problems can turn a validly formed argument into a fallacy. In the informal fallacy of CUM HOC ERGO PROPTER HOC ('With this, therefore because of this') a false cause is imagined between events:

   "Every day I boil my kettle." "Hey! There are no elephants around here!"
   "Wow! How about that! Boiling my kettle keeps elephants away!"

The study of fallacies is important for the aspiring logician, and examples will appear throughout this book. Sometimes they are introduced into arguments by mistake; but they are also wielded by unscrupulous orators to win disputes by nefarious means.

Smart logicians can quickly identify the fallacies fed to them every day by parents, politicians, pundits, advertisers, and teenagers —all those who may have a vested interest in their deception.

REASONING
elementary, my dear

There are four main ways to form a logical conclusion.

DEDUCTIVE REASONING moves from the general to the particular, producing a necessary conclusion whose truth follows from that of the premises. It is the motor behind the *syllogism (see p. 14)*, other instruments of traditional logic, and computers.

1. *Mythical animals do not really exist.* ✓
2. *Werewolves are mythical animals.* ✓
∴ *Werewolves do not really exist.* ✓

Given the truth of the assumptions, a valid deduction will always lead to a true conclusion.

INDUCTIVE REASONING begins with the particular and proceeds to the general. Things are observed, then a rule or cause is proposed to account for them. This allows for innumerable general laws to be formulated which facilitate our daily lives, and permit science to advance by hypotheses, tests, and theories.

1. *I see an apple falling from a tree.* ✓
2. *I see it happen again and again.* ✓
3. *I form a hypothesis to explain it.* ✓
4. *Further experiments support my hypothesis and it is elevated to a theory, part of a law.* ✓

The conclusion is only probable, rather than certain, which is why, strictly speaking, no scientific theory is regarded as being true.

ABDUCTIVE REASONING infers the truth of the best explanation for a set of facts even if that explanation includes unobserved elements. It is the process of making educated guesses at why some given set or circumstances is the case. As such it benefits from the application of *Occam's Razor (see p. 39)*. Diagnosticians and detectives commonly employ abductive reasoning.

1. *If it rains, the grass becomes wet.* ✓
2. *The grass is wet.* ✓
∴ *It is most likely that it rained.* ✓

The conclusion is probable but not exclusive; someone might have watered the lawn.

ANALOGICAL REASONING transfers information from a particular source to a particular target. It plays a central role in problem solving and cognitive perception by using comparison, similarities, and correspondences. It is always preceded by inductive reasoning:

1. *Many objects have been observed to share certain characteristics.* ✓
2. *We induce a class of these things by their common characteristics and name it 'apples'.* ✓
3. *We observe a target which shares characteristics we have found to be typical of apples.* ✓

4. *We reason analogically that this is also an apple!* ✓

The conclusion is only probable: it could be a plastic apple.

Analogical reasoning helps us observe patterns in the world and make on-the-spot decisions every day. However, if the wrong patterns are used, it falls into the **ANALOGICAL FALLACY** (see p. 34).

STATEMENTS AND ARGUMENTS
saying what's what

For the Greek philosopher Aristotle [384–322 BC], the basic building blocks of argument were *statements*, made up of *subjects* and *predicates*, i.e. what we are talking about and what we are saying about it. Today, logicians recognise a number of basic types of statement:

1. **PREDICATIVE STATEMENT: S IS P.** '*Cats are mammals*'. The most simple statement, where S is the subject and P is the predicate.

2. **CONJUNCTIVE STATEMENT: P AND Q.** '*Animals and reptiles*', as in **S IS P AND Q:** '*Crocodiles are animals and reptiles*'. Note that the predications can be separated out, e.g. '*S is P. S is (also) Q, etc*'.

3. **DISJUNCTIVE STATEMENT: P OR Q:** There are three kinds:
   i. **S OR Q (OR R OR …) IS P.** '*Either you or I (or Balthezar, or Mavis, or Myrtle, or …) will win*'. Can extend to cover all options.
   ii. **S IS P OR Q.** '*A person is dead or alive.*'
   iii. **S IS P, OR T IS Q.** '*Either I'll win or you'll do a headstand.*'

4. **CONDITIONAL/HYPOTHETICAL STATEMENT: IF S, THEN P.** '*If the sun shines, the beach will be busy*'. The first part is called the *antecedent*, the second the *consequent*. The logical/material link between them is called the *nexus*.

   THE NEXUS: The truth of '*If Robert has a vision all will be well*' depends on the connection between Robert's visions and subsequent events. If this nexus does not hold, then the statement will be unsound and produce the informal fallacy of the **FLAWED NEXUS**. E.g., '*If music is* *playing, it is snowing'* is fallacious since, even if it happens to be true, there is no logical or substantive connection (nexus) between music and snow. (*Conditionals behave differently in formal logic, see p.50.*)

5. COMPARATIVE STATEMENT: **A** IS LIKE **B** IN THIS RESPECT. *'Tangerines are like small oranges'.* This is *analogical reasoning (p.7)*.

In comparative statements, beware the **ANALOGICAL FALLACY**, where someone mistakenly assumes that, because two or more things are similar in one way, they must be similar in others (*see p. 34*).

Two or more statements can be combined to form *arguments*, which proceed from the known (the premises) to the previously-unknown (the conclusion). A common example is:

THE ARGUMENT FROM UNIVERSAL TO PARTICULAR.
ALL ⇒ SOME / ONE. *'All meerkats are cool, therefore this meerkat is cool'.*
If a universal statement is true, a particular version with the same subject and predicate is also true.

While it is valid to move from universal to particular, the reverse, **THE MOVE FROM PARTICULAR TO UNIVERSAL,** where a case or group of cases infer a general rule, is an informal fallacy of **UNJUSTIFIED INDUCTION**:

> *Many politicians break their campaign promises* ∴ *All politicians are liars.*

All politicians may indeed be liars; but we can't prove it like this.

"... and on that you have my word."

PROPOSITIONS
value, quality, modality, quantity

In his logical writings—called collectively the *Organon* (lit., the 'instrument' or 'tool')—Aristotle set out the basic theory and practice of a far-reaching analysis of statements, their valid interactions, and their relationship to the realities they signify. Every classical Aristotelian proposition has four technical *characteristics*:

1. **VALUE**: *true* or *false*.

2. **QUALITY**: *affirmative* or *negative*. 'All stoats are mammals' is an affirmative proposition, while 'No stoats are reptiles' is a negative one.

3. **MODALITY**: *categorical* or *modal*. A statement of absolute fact such as 'Ants are insects' is a categorical proposition, while an *obligation*, such as 'Politicians should serve the public good', or a *contingency*, such as 'Politicians may be corrupt', are modal propositions.

4. **QUANTITY**: *universal* or *particular*. A proposition such as 'All mammals are red' or 'No mammal is blue' is said to be 'universal', whereas a partial proposition such as 'Some skunks smell nice', or a particular proposition such as 'René is a skunk' is 'particular'.

So, for example, 'Every statement is either true or false' is true, affirmative, categorical, and universal; while '... except some paradoxes, which may be neither!' is true, negative, modal, and particular.

10

INTENTION AND IMPOSITION
sense and sensibility

Propositions in traditional logic are made up of *terms*, each of which has two possible *intentions* and three possible *impositions*:

INTENTION refers to the use of a term with regard to logical function:

1. FIRST INTENTION *refers to the real world* ('Slugs are slimy').
2. SECOND INTENTION *refers to the reflexive use of terms as regards their logical status or function* ('Slugs is a term referring to a class of beings').

A lion is a feline.   Feline is a genus.   ∴ A lion is a genus.   Er, no!

This is the fallacy of **SHIFT OF INTENTION**; a cat is a *member* of a genus.

IMPOSITION refers to the use of a term with regard to language itself.

0. NO IMPOSITION *refers to phonetics or spelling, ignoring the meaning of the term* ('Slugs has five letters').
1. FIRST IMPOSITION *refers to the real world* ('Slugs are slimy').
2. SECOND IMPOSITION *refers reflexively to the word as a word* ('Slugs is the subject of the statement "Slugs are slimy"').

The fallacy of **SHIFT OF IMPOSITION** occurs when we wrongly use the same term in two or more impositions:

Jupiter is a planet (first imposition). Planet is a word of two syllables (no imposition).
∴ Jupiter is a word of two syllables (false, whichever imposition is understood).

First intention and first imposition are the province of the everyday use of language. Logic is the art of analysing second intentions; grammar is the art of analysing second impositions.

DEFINING TERMS
distribution, substance, and accident

Clearly defined terms are an essential part of the art of reasoning, while unclear or undefined terms are fatal to clear argumentation. Traditional logic crucially distinguishes between two types of term:

1. **DISTRIBUTED** terms cover their entire class ('all hens', 'humankind').

2. **UNDISTRIBUTED** terms cover part of a class ('some ducks', 'a fox').

Pay close attention to the distribution of terms, as sneaky changes in distribution can invalidate an argument (*see p. 23*).

A second crucial distinction is between **SUBSTANCE** and **ACCIDENT**.

1. **SUBSTANCE** is that which exists in itself ('frog', 'mountain'). If any aspect of a substance is taken away, it ceases to be what it is.

2. **ACCIDENT** is that which exists in something other than itself ('sat', 'red'). Accidents are qualities or states of being in a particular way.

So, in defining a 'bird', we may mention wings and feathers as defining characteristics, 'substances', but must omit 'green and blue', as an 'accident' which only some birds have. Take another example:

The tall Greek woman stood poised on the balcony in a long black ballgown.

Here the substance is '*woman*', and remains so regardless of what accidents are predicated of it and however much the sentence is rephrased or simplified.

Confusing substance and accident can lead to absurdities, as Lewis

Carroll [1832–1898] demonstrates in *Alice's Adventures in Wonderland*:

> "Well! I've often seen a cat without a grin," thought Alice, "but a grin without a cat! It's the most curious thing I ever saw in my life!"

Here, the term '*grin*' is actually an accident disguised as a substance. An accident cannot remain when the substance has vanished. When we assert that it does, we commit the formal fallacy of CONFUSING SUBSTANCE AND ACCIDENT (*not to be confused with* THE FALLACY OF ACCIDENT, *which is a sub-category—see p. 32*).

Above: In Alice's Adventure's in Wonderland the Cheshire Cat can appear and disappear at will, sometimes leaving its grin behind.

Substance, plus the nine different types of accident, make up Aristotle's *Ten Categories of Being*:

1. **SUBSTANCE** ('horse', 'tree')
2. **QUANTITY** ('fast', 'tall');
3. **QUALITY** ('white', 'lovely');
4. **RELATION** ('cousin', 'greater');
5. **ACTION** ('cuts', 'runs');
6. **PASSION** ('is cut', 'is run');
7. **TIME** ('yesterday', 'soon');
8. **LOCATION** ('in the car', 'here');
9. **POSTURE** ('lies', 'sits');
10. **HABIT** ('shod', 'armed').

Some of Aristotle's categories may seem dated today, but they still demonstrate an important principle. You can have a cat without a grin, but you can't have a grin without a cat!

SYLLOGISMS
are you in or out?

Aristotle believed that all categorical logical deductions (i.e. those dealing with general or universal terms like 'women', 'fishing', and 'freedom') were reducible to three-sentence structures called *syllogisms* (from Gr. *syllogismos*, deduction or reasoning about multiple terms). These consist of a major premise, a minor premise, and a conclusion:

EXAMPLE OF A SYLLOGISM

1. *All men are mortal*   *Major Premise*
2. *Socrates is a man*   *Minor Premise*
∴ *Socrates is mortal*   *Conclusion*

Strictly speaking, 'Socrates' here stands for 'the class of all things that are Socrates'. The syllogism can produce necessary truths:

A. *If the premises are true,* and B. *The form of syllogism is valid,* then
C. *The conclusion will be true.*

The three propositions of the syllogism have three *terms*: *major*, *minor*, and *middle*:

The MAJOR TERM *is the predicate of the conclusion:* 'mortal'
The MINOR TERM *is the subject of the conclusion:* 'Socrates'
The MIDDLE TERM *is held in common by both premises:* 'men'.

Each term appears twice in the whole syllogism, with the middle term linking the two premises but disappearing in the conclusion. The middle term *must* be distributed ('all men') in one or both of the premises, rather than being specific ('a man') or limited ('some men'), otherwise we fall into the formal fallacy of **THE UNDISTRIBUTED MIDDLE TERM**. So, in the example:

1. *All rich people are taxable people.* ✓
2. *Some taxable people are poor;* ✓
∴. *All rich people are poor.* ✗

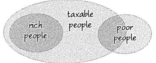

the middle term 'taxable' is undistributed since it does not in either instance encompass the total field of all taxable entities. Syllogisms with undistributed middles do not prove anything:

1. *Some violent anarchists are animal lovers.* ✓
2. *All cat lovers are animal lovers.* ✓
∴. *All cat lovers are violent anarchists* ✗

An easy way to differentiate between syllogisms is to draw a logical diagram. In many cases a simple glance can quickly expose a fallacy.

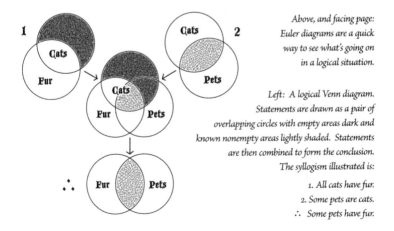

Above, and facing page: Euler diagrams are a quick way to see what's going on in a logical situation.

Left: A logical Venn diagram. Statements are drawn as a pair of overlapping circles with empty areas dark and known nonempty areas lightly shaded. Statements are then combined to form the conclusion. The syllogism illustrated is:

1. *All cats have fur.*
2. *Some pets are cats.*
∴ *Some pets have fur.*

A SQUARE OF OPPOSITIONS
all, some, or none

In his work *On Interpretation*, Aristotle describes a symmetry between statements of differing quality and quantity. Known as the *Table of Oppositions*, it has been shown as a fourfold diagram (*opposite*) since the work of Boethius [c. 480–524]. The two possible qualities (affirmative and negative) are multiplied with the two possible quantities (universal and particular) to get four simple types of categorical proposition.

In medieval times, mnemonic vowels were assigned to the four kinds of statements, derived from the Latin: A and I are the first two vowels in *affirmo*, 'I affirm', while E and O come from *nego*, 'I deny'.

The Table shows the hidden relationships between various types of proposition. In summary, these relationships are:

CONTRARIES: *The upper statements are contrary; both cannot be true.*

CONTRADICTORIES: *The diagonal lines show statements which cannot both be true and cannot both be false.*

SUBCONTRARIES: *The lower two propositions do not necessarily contradict each other, but cannot both be false.*

SUBALTERNS and SUPERALTERNS: *The two universals at the top of the square automatically entail their lower counterparts.*

For Aristotle, and in traditional logic, all statements, universal (A and E) and particular (I and O), imply the existence of their subjects. So in the example on the opposite page the statement '*All words are wise*' implies that words exist (*this is not the case in modern logic, see p. 19*).

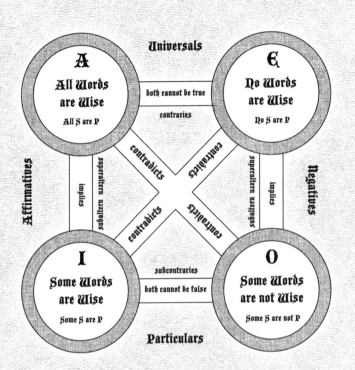

The Medieval Square of Oppositions

Two-way diagonals connect contradictories: so if A is true, O is false, and vice versa (same for E and I). One-way horizontals connect contraries: so if A or I is true, E or O is false, respectively. However, if E or O is false, we don't know the value of A or I, respectively. One-way verticals connect superalterns with subalterns, so A and E imply I and O, but not vice-versa (medieval logicians called this rule Dictum de Omni et Nullo—whatever is affirmed or denied of a logical whole must also be affirmed or denied of its parts).

SYLLOGISTIC FALLACIES
misdeductions

A syllogism can go wrong in many ways. It may have four terms (QUATERNIO TERMINORUM), but even with three, out of 256 possible types, only 24 are valid in classical logic, and just 15 in modern logic. Using the vowels for the four types of proposition in the *Table of Opposites* (*pages 16–17*), medieval logicians devised mnemonics to learn these by heart:

BARBARA AAA1	CESARE EAE2	DATISI AII3	CALEMES AEE4
CELARENT EAE1	CAMESTRES AEE2	DISAMIS IAI3	DIMATIS IAI4
DARII AII1	FESTINO EIO2	FERISON EIO3	FRESISON EIO4
FERIO EIO1	BAROCO AOO2	BOCARDO OAO3	CALEMOS AEO4
BARBARI AAI1	CESARO EAO2	FELAPTON EAO3	FESAPO EAO4
CELARONT EAO1	CAMESTROS AEO2	DARAPTI AAI3	BAMALIP AAI4

Syllogistic formal fallacies can be hard to spot. Here are three *Invalid Combinations of Positive and Negative Statements*:

EXCLUSIVE PREMISES: If both premises are negative, no connection is established between the major and minor terms.

> 1. No *aliens are human.* [E] ✓
> 2. No *humans have three eyes.* [E] ✓
> Therefore, *all aliens have three eyes.* [A] ✗

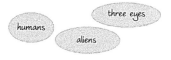

AFFIRMATIVE CONCLUSION FROM A NEGATIVE PREMISE: If either premise is negative, the conclusion must also be negative.

> 1. All *fights are trouble.* [A] ✓
> 2. No *trouble is worth dying for.* [E] ✓
> ∴ All *fights are worth dying for.* [A] ✗

The correct conclusion should be: No *fight is worth dying for.*

Negative Conclusion from Affirmative Premises: If both premises are affirmative, the conclusion must also be affirmative.

1. *All cows need grass.* [A] ✓
2. *All grass needs rain.* [A] ✓
∴ *No cow needs rain.* [E] ✗

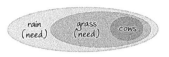

Which is untrue; the conclusion is: *Therefore, All cows need rain.*

There are also three *Fallacies of Distribution*: We've already seen the fallacy of the **Undistributed Middle Term** (*see p. 15*). A second rule is that no term may be distributed in the conclusion if it is undistributed in its premise (although it can move from distributed to undistributed). Breaking this gives us the **Illicit Treatment of the Major Term:**

1. *All evil things are bad for you.* [A] ✓
2. *No chemicals are evil things.* [E] ✓
∴ *No chemicals are bad for you.* [E] ✗

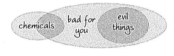

No! Some chemicals could still be bad for you, despite not being evil.

The third fallacy is the **Illicit Treatment of the Minor Term:**

1. *All cannibals are meat-eaters.* [A] ✓
2. *All cannibals are murderers.* [A] ✓
∴ *All meat-eaters are murderers.* [A] ✗

Neither premise has '*all meat-eaters*', so it can't be in the conclusion.

In modern Boolean logic, universal statements (*All fairies have wings*) do *not* imply the existence of their subjects, while particular statements (*some fairies have wings*) do. To assume the existence of the subjects of universal statements is to commit the **Existential Fallacy.** Disallowing it shaves the nine greyed syllogisms from the 24 opposite.

MODUS PONENS
everyday and direct

A simple and powerful form of deductive argument was identified by the Stoic logician Chrysippus of Soli [c.280–c.205 BC]. It is known as *modus ponens* ('the way of adding on'), and we use it every day:

> *If P, then Q; P; therefore Q.*

Here it is again, in a slightly expanded form:

> 1. *If P is true, then Q is also true.* 2. *P is true.* ∴ *Therefore Q is true.*

> 1. *If I touch the bubble, it will burst.* 2. *I touched the bubble.* ∴ *It burst.*

Modus ponens is a powerful logical tool. Everyday examples of *modus ponens* don't immediately resemble the template above, but by using *expansion (see p. 24)* and examining the *nexus (see p.8)* we can detect the validity-preserving *modus* hiding in everyday speech:

> *All fish can swim, so this fish can swim.*

can be rephrased as a classic modus ponens:

> 1. *If it is true that this is a fish (If P), then it is true that it can swim (then Q).*
> 2. *This is a fish (P is true).*
> ∴ *This fish can swim (Therefore Q is true).*

Modus ponens is also iterative; arguments can be built on top of one another *ad infinitum*. The following argument, for example, is valid:

> *All logicians are clever. All clever people need pencils.*
> *Therefore, all logicians need pencils.*

We can use expansion (*see p. 24*) to show that this syllogism in *Barbara* consists of two *modus ponens* arguments. Firstly:

1. *If it is true that there are logicians (If P), then they are clever (then Q).*
2. *Logicians exist (P).* ∴ *They are clever (Therefore, Q).*

where the last two parts of the argument are implied rather than stated, as statements of mere existence often are. And secondly:

1. *If clever people exist (If Q), then they need pencils (then R).*
2. *Clever people exist (Q).* ∴ *They need pencils (∴ R).*

Iteration gives rise to *sorites*, a long chain of arguments attached one to the other. It also gives rise to *sorites* paradoxes (*see p. 44*), one of the most intractable types of logical problem.

The *modus ponens* has an important formal fallacy of its own:

AFFIRMING THE CONSEQUENT (the consequent is the 'then' part of the first line of the argument). Here, instead of arguing (validly):

1. *If P, then Q.*   2. *P.*   ∴ *Therefore Q,*

it argues (invalidly):

1. *If P, then Q.*   2. *Q.*   ∴ *Therefore P.*

1. *If I touch the bubble, it will burst.*
2. *The bubble burst.*   ∴ *I touched it.*

This is incorrect; the bubble may have burst for any number of other reasons. This fallacy often shows up in political discourse:

1. *If someone is a terrorist, they will be critical of our government.*
2. *This man is critical of our government;*   ∴ *This man is a terrorist.*

MODUS TOLLENS
everyday and indirect

Modus tollens signifies 'the way of taking away'; it is the negative cousin of *modus ponens*, and takes the form:

    1. If P then Q.   2. Not Q.   Therefore, not P.

    1. *If I touch the bubble, it will burst.*
    2. *The bubble didn't burst.* ∴ *I didn't touch it.*

The validity of *modus tollens* relies on the fact that, if a cause always leads to an effect, then if you don't have the effect then you don't have the cause either. (As with all conditionals, always check the *nexus, p. 8*.)

The *modus tollens* also has a nasty formal fallacy of its own:

DENYING THE ANTECEDENT (the antecedent is the 'If P' part). Here, instead of the valid version above, we get the sneaky:

    1. If P, then Q.   2. Not P, ∴ Not Q,

    1. *If I touch the bubble, it will burst.*
    2. *I didn't touch it.* ∴ *It didn't burst.*

which is again very useful for political purposes:

    1. *If a man is a terrorist, he will be critical of our government.*
    2. *This man is not a terrorist;*
    ∴ *He won't be critical of our government.*

"NOT SO FAST! HOW DO WE KNOW YOU'RE NOT TERRORISTS WITH WEAPONS OF MASS DESTRUCTION?"

EDUCTION
rearranging propositions

Sometimes things need rephrasing. In *Alice's Adventures in Wonderland*, the March Hare tells Alice that she should say what she means:

"I do", Alice hastily replied; "at least — at least I mean what I say — that's the same thing, you know." "Not the same thing a bit!" said the Hatter. "Why, you might just as well say that 'I see what I eat' is the same thing as 'I eat what I see'!"

CONVERSION reverses a proposition, turning the subject into the predicate and vice versa, e.g. "*I am Sam = Sam I am*". But watch out:

All men are monkeys = All monkeys are men

demonstrates the FALLACY OF FALSE CONVERSION, as the term '*monkeys*' has become illegally distributed. It has gone from a 'some' to an 'all'.

In OBVERSION we change the quality of a statement from affirmative to negative (or vice-versa), and the predicate to its complement (non-):

Bucephalus is a horse = Bucephalus is not a non-horse,

taking care not to confuse "*a non-horse*" with "*not a horse*", or we will be committing the FALLACY OF ILLICIT OBVERSION.

CONTRAPOSITION reverses and negates: *All sharks are killers = All non-killers are non-sharks*". It is valid for A ('all') and O ('some ... not'), and invalid for E ('no') and I ('some') propositions (*see p. 16*).

LOGICAL EXPANSION
drawing out hidden logic

Annoyingly (for logicians at least), many premises vital to arguments are completely omitted in everyday speech, both on the assumption that they are already understood, and to keep sentences short. As a result, most arguments bear little resemblance to the traditional forms of deduction. *Logical expansion*, however, restates an argument to reveal its hidden assumptions and make explicit its logical content. It is an essential tool for the aspiring logician to help discover and clarify the errors often lurking in an argument. Consider this one:

> *Flipper is a mammal because he is a dolphin.*

In traditional logic an abridged argument like this is known as an *enthymeme*. It is seen as valid if it can be expanded into a valid syllogism (*see p. 190*) even if it leaves out a large number of the elements of the syllogism itself. Of all the possible syllogisms which may be created from an enthymeme, only *one* need be valid for the enthymeme to be valid (*see too p. 240*). In this case, the enthymeme may clearly be expanded to a syllogism through the addition of the minor premise:

> *All dolphins are mammals.*

Expansions often reveal logical errors which can be developed into useful lines of attack.

Consider the latent assumptions in this example:

> **MR. RABBIT:** *Fellow council members, are you blind? Of course Mr. Fox's conservation policies will favor carnivores, since he himself is a carnivore.*

which may be expanded thus:

1. *Mr. Fox is a carnivore.*
2. *All carnivores support policies which favor carnivores.*
∴ *Mr. Fox's conservation policies will favor carnivores.*

The argument may now be attacked based on the latent premise (2); if it is false, then the argument is unsound:

> MR. FOX: *This is illogical nonsense! Most carnivores are decent, fair, hardworking folk who support balanced conservation policies that favor the entire forest, carnivores and non-carnivores alike. Your latent premise is false. Your argument does not hold.*

Words like 'since' and 'because' often indicate the presence of a hidden premise. Premises may only be added if they are implicit in the original argument; you cannot add extraneous material. Spotting intruders is not always easy, but there are two conservation rules for logical expansion which can be very helpful:

> TRUTH-VALUES MUST BE CONSERVED. *However we rearrange the statement 'Flipper is a mammal because he is a dolphin', we can never state that 'Flipper is not a dolphin' (changed truth value).*

> DISTRIBUTION MUST BE CONSERVED. *We cannot go from a distributed to an undistributed term—from 'All dolphins are mammals' to 'Some dolphins are mammals'—or vice versa (changed distribution).*

DILEMMAS
caught between two horns

Have you ever been impaled on the 'horns' of a *dilemma*, forced to choose between two or more mutually exclusive and undesirable options? A *logical dilemma* is a complex syllogism in three parts:

1. *A Disjunctive minor premise, (either ... or); the 'horns'*
2. *A Compound hypothetical major premise, (if ... then; if ... then); the 'conjuncts'*
∴ *A Simple or disjunctive conclusion, (either 'therefore, P' or 'therefore, either P or Q')*

So, for example, take this famous dilemma adapted from Aristotle:

1. *Either we ought to practice logic, or we ought not.*
2. *If we ought, then we ought; if we ought not, then we still ought (because we need logic to justify why we ought not).* ∴ *We ought to practice logic.*

The 'then' consequences in the second line are the 'conjuncts', and if any are false, the whole dilemma is false. The final choice between the conjuncts can be *simple*, as above, or *disjunctive/complex*. The Christian father Tertullian used the following complex dilemma to try to persuade the Stoic emperor Marcus Aurelius to stop persecuting Christians:

1. *Either the Christians have committed crimes or they have not.*
2. *If they have, your refusal to permit a public enquiry is irrational; if they have not, your punishing them is unjust.*
∴ *You are either irrational or unjust.*

The initial *disjunct* may present more than two options: if three, we are dealing with a *trilemma*, and if four or more, a *polylemma*.

The 'horns' in any kind of *-lemma* must represent exclusive options: if there are any other possibilities, then the whole formulation is false, and falls into the fallacy of IMPERFECT DISJUNCTION OF THE MINOR PREMISE, commonly known as a FALSE DILEMMA or FALSE CHOICE.

For example, Archbishop John Morton was put in charge of levying taxes on the nobility for Henry VII. When reminded that some of the nobility might not be able to afford to pay, he replied that

> Either the nobles live lavishly, in which case they can be taxed; or they appear poor, in which case they are living frugally and must have savings which can be taxed.

Expanded to a full dilemma, the conclusion would be 'all may be taxed'. 'Morton's Fork' ignores the very real possibility that those who appear poor might actually be poor, and so offers a false choice.

Dilemmas can counter other dilemmas. The sophist Protagoras taught his student Euathlus rhetoric on condition that Euathlus would pay him upon winning his first court-case, but eventually Protagoras tired of waiting for his fee and decided to sue him, reasoning:

1. Either Euathlus will win the case or lose.
2. If he wins, he will have to pay me because he owed me my fee subject to winning his first case; if he loses, he will have to pay me because I will have successfully sued him for the pay he owes me.
∴ Euathlus will have to pay me.

Euathlus, however, reasoned to opposite conclusions as follows:

1. Either I will win the case or lose.
2. If I win, I will not have to pay, because the court will have found in favor of me; if I lose, I will not have to pay because I will have lost my first court case.
∴ Either way I will not have to pay Protagoras.

DEALING WITH DILEMMAS
go between, grasp, or counter

Politicians and parents regularly use abbreviated dilemmas to present complex circumstances as clean-cut either-or situations involving only two choices (especially when selling the lesser of two evils):

Either we record everyone's phone calls, or the terrorists grow stronger.

There are various ways of dealing with such insidious devices:

ESCAPING BETWEEN THE HORNS. Are the two either-or options really exclusive? If you can find a third option then you can 'go between the horns of the dilemma'. In Plato's *Meno* (80e), Meno proposes that it is impossible to learn anything new:

A man cannot search for what he knows (since he knows it, there is no need to search); nor for what he doesn't know (for he doesn't know what to look for).

Socrates posits a third option: new knowledge is actually *recollection*. He escapes the dilemma by denying the original options are exclusive.

GRASPING THE HORNS OF THE DILEMMA. If you can show that one or both of the major premises is false, i.e. the nexus of the hypothetical statement (the 'if ... then' part) is not valid (*see p. 8*), then there is no necessary connection between antecedent and consequent:

1. *People are either good, or they're bad.*
2. *If they're good, then we don't need laws to deter crime.*
   If they're bad, then laws to deter crime won't work.
∴ *Either way, laws to deter crime are useless.*

In this classic dilemma, a favorite of anarchists, some may agree with the first premise, but the second is flimsy. By grasping this horn firmly and showing its shortcomings we may counter it thus:

Laws do not deter crime, but fear of punishment does — in bad people, average people, and even in quite good people. So the second premise is wrong. Laws to deter crime are useful, as they threaten punishment to those who might otherwise commit crimes.

COUNTERDILEMMA. The most stylish and rhetorically-effective method of dealing with a dilemma is to counter, or rebut, it. Ideally, this should be done with a new dilemma constructed from the same premises as the old one, but with a new and opposite conclusion (*as shown on page 27*). A good example is the ancient Greek story of the mother who begs her son not to enter politics:

1. *If you enter politics, you will either act justly or unjustly.*
2. *If you act unjustly, the gods will hate you; but if you act justly, men will hate you.*
∴ *Entering politics guarantees that you will be hated.*

Her son counters her, effortlessly finding a valid reversed conclusion without changing the value of the premises:

1. *If I enter politics, I will either act justly or unjustly.*
2. *If I act unjustly, men will love me; but if justly, the gods will love me.*
∴ *Entering politics guarantees that I will be loved!*

LINGUISTIC FALLACIES
spoken with a forked tongue

Aristotle and his followers codified a group of informal fallacies known as fallacies *in dictione* (Lat. 'in language'), resulting from sloppy language:

AMPHIBOLY (Gr. 'thrown both ways'): Sometimes, a proposition can be read in two or more ways, and it is impossible to tell which is meant:

> *One morning I shot an elephant in my pyjamas.*
> *How he got into my pyjamas, I don't know.* - Groucho Marx

This fallacy is rarely wielded deliberately; it's mostly inadvertent.

COMPOSITION: This fallacy occurs properties of constituent elements of a whole are illicitly attributed to the whole itself:

> 1. *Hydrogen and oxygen are both gases at room temperature;* ✓
> 2. *Water is made up of hydrogen and oxygen;* ✓
> ∴ *Water is a gas at room temperature.* ✗

DIVISION: In contrast to composition, this fallacy occurs when the properties of a whole are attributed to its parts:

> *Nine plus nine is eighteen, which is an even number.* ✓
> *Since eighteen is even, nine must be even as well.* ✗

This is common in statistical interpretation, where it can seem that a case that stands out from a statistical group is responsible for what is in fact due to the entire group. It's not the last roll of the dice which loses a gambler their money, but all the rolls weighed up cumulatively.

Ambiguity can arise from distributive and collective predication to groups, so '*People drink more water than elephants*' is true collectively but false distributively. A composition fallacy arises in going from the distributive to the collective sense; division goes the other way.

EQUIVOCATION: Some words have two or more meanings. This fallacy occurs when multiple meanings crop up in a single argument:

1. *Fluff is light.* ✓
2. *Light travels faster than anything else in the universe.* ✓
∴ *Fluff travels faster than anything else in the universe.* ✗

VERBAL FORM: Sometimes the form of words can suggest equivalence where there is none. Take the words 'inaudible', 'inadmissible', and 'inflammable': the prefix 'in' in the first two cases signifies 'not', but in the third case means 'extremely'. This fallacy often takes subtle forms arising from similarities in phrasing (especially sloppy use of verbal tenses) that hide different meanings:

1. *Those who eat the least are the most hungry.* ✓
2. *Hungry people eat the most.* ✓
∴ *Those who eat the least eat the most.* ✗

The problem here is the English tendency to use the present tense to signify both the future and habitual past action. Instead:

1. *Those who* HAVE EATEN *the least are the most hungry.* ✓
2. *Hungry people* WILL *eat the most.* ✓
∴ *Those who have eaten the least will eat the most.* ✓

31

NON-LINGUISTIC FALLACIES
built on false assumptions

The informal Aristotelian 'non-linguistic' (*extra dictionem*) fallacies all contain some false assumption. They tend to be trickier to spot than the fallacies *in dictione*, where the problems are purely linguistic.

ACCIDENT FALLACY: Much everyday human thinking relies on general statements (commonplaces or 'rules-of-thumb'). But these always have exceptions. This fallacy occurs when the exceptions are used to attack the validity of the rule (i.e. accident is confused with substance, hence the name, *see p. 189*). For example:

1. *Humans are rational animals (generally a useful rule of thumb).* ✓
2. *Some humans are dead (also true, but …).* ✓
∴ *Dead people are rational.* ✗

This is a perverse reading of the first premise as a categorical statement rather than a rule of thumb; put another way, it confuses substance (human being) with accident (the state of being dead).

SECUNDUM QUID (literally, 'in this respect'): This fallacy occurs when it is assumed that a statement which is true in certain respects is true in all respects, or in other irrelevant respects. It is also known as 'converse accident' (as it reverses the accident fallacy) or 'hasty generalization':

1. *I have been to Paris three times, and* ✓
2. *Each time I was there someone was rude to me.* ✓
∴ *Parisians are rude.* ✗

Parisians may be rude, or maybe only three of them are.

FALSE CAUSE: This fallacy imputes causation to a relationship which may not involve any. It is especially popular with amateur moralists:

Firearms are EVIL; they KILL people!

This argument confuses an accident attendant on firearms (that they are used to kill) with their essential nature. A false cause is thus created for asserting that they are evil, rather than the correct conclusion, which is that some people do evil things with firearms.

Other common forms are **CUM HOC ERGO PROPTER HOC** (*see p. 5*) and its sibling, **POST HOC ERGO PROPTER HOC** (Lat. 'after this, therefore because of this'), which assume that, because two events occur simultaneously (cum hoc) or sequentially (post hoc) they must be causally linked:

Last year, poverty rose in the same regions where welfare spending rose. Amazingly, it seems that welfare spending increases poverty! (CUM HOC)

We did the rain-dance and OMG it rained! This stuff works! (POST HOC)

He was elected President, and car companies went bust. His fault! (POST HOC)

The fallacy of **COMPLEX QUESTION** smuggles one or more assumptions into a question and then demands a single answer. This is a favorite fallacy for courtroom entrapment:

PROSECUTOR: *When did you meet the woman you would later murder?*

A plaintiff would be extremely foolish to answer this. The appropriate response is to demand a proper question.

MORE INFORMAL FALLACIES
devious devices

Some logical fallacies are really rhetorical tricks. Studying these fiendish figures can arm you against the slippery sleight-of-tongue wielded served up by rhetoricians of all stamps every day.

THE ANALOGICAL FALLACY assumes that because two or more things are similar in one way, they must be similar in other ways:

> 1. The universe is like a watch. ✓ 2. A watch is made by a watchmaker. ✓
> ∴ Therefore the universe must have a universe-maker. ×

An analogical argument is only valid if there is an explicit premise stating that the things being compared are similar in the relevant respects. If that premise is true then it also sound; if not, it is valid but unsound. False analogies can be exposed by exposing differences between the analogous terms, using *reductio ad absurdum* (see p.38).

> 1. The universe is like a watch. ✓ 2. A watch can give you an itchy wrist. ✓
> ∴ Therefore the universe can give you an itchy wrist. ×

BEGGING THE QUESTION (*circular reasoning*) is a sneaky fallacy that occurs whenever the argument uses the conclusion as a premise. It assumes what it is trying to prove before it has proven it!

> AMY: *God exists because the Bible says so.*
> BILL: *But how do you know the Bible is true?*
> AMY: *The Bible IS the word of God; it's obvious.*

Such reasoning is not actually invalid but it begs the listener to ask the appropriate question concerning circularity:

BILL: *You can't use the Bible as a proof of God's existence when the only proof of its truth is that it comes from God, whose existence you have yet to prove.*

SHIFTING THE BURDEN OF PROOF is a favorite of every lawyer who can get away with it, as the burden of proof is an important component of the logic used in courtrooms:

PROSECUTOR: *Did you not visit the store beforehand to plan your robbery?*
DEFENDANT: *I visited the store, but only to do some shopping.*
PROSECUTOR: *But can you prove that you were not planning a robbery?*
DEFENDANT: *No, but ... um ....*

The fallacy demands that someone prove that they were *not* doing something (often impossible). Medieval logicians formulated a rule to guard against this: *onus probandi incumbit ei qui dicit, non ei qui negat* ('the burden of proof is on the one who makes the accusation, not on the one who denies it'). Our defendant should have responded:

DEFENDANT: *You have no proof that I was planning a robbery. There is no need for me to prove my innocence, which is assumed.*

FALSE CHOICE is a pernicious fallacy where limited options are given as the sole possibilities (where in fact more exist):

Every nation in every region now has a decision to make: either you are with us, or you are with the terrorists. – George W. Bush, Sept. 20, 2001

Deal with this type of false dichotomy in the same way that you might a dilemma (*see p. 28*), either by going between its horns and demonstrating a valid third position (e.g. that it's possible not to be a supporter of either Bush or the terrorists), or by grasping the horns (e.g. showing that both sides are actually 'terrorists').

FALLACIES OF MISDIRECTION
now watch closely

———————————

Some fallacies ignore the argument rather than refuting it honestly.
These are forms of IGNORATIO ELENCHI ('ignorance of the argument').

THE IRRELEVANT THESIS is a tricky fallacy. It makes a valid point, but fails
to address the issue in question.

> INTERVIEWER: '*Mr President, is it not true that under your term of office
> poverty has risen by 20%?*'
> PRESIDENT: '*In my term of office, we have in fact seen record corporate profits.*'

This fallacy is popular with politicians who wish to avoid
answering a question; instead they deliberately miss the point.

THE RED HERRING tries to divert the course of argument by introducing
irrelevant material. For maximum effect, the red herring should be
something which is likely to get a strong emotional response.

> PROSECUTOR: '*Is it not true, Senator, that you expropriated enormous amounts
> of money from military contracts over the course of decades for your personal use?*'
> SENATOR: '*I served in the military, I love the military, and as far as I am
> concerned anyone who attacks the integrity of our military is a traitor.*'

Hearing this indignant speech, the audience may become roused
by patriotic feelings, while the senator has ignored the question,
and helped the audience to forget it was asked at all.

THE STRAW MAN ARGUMENT is a trick for dealing with an opponent who has
strong support for their position. It takes the form of a deliberate

misrepresentation of their position, which is easy to knock down. At the great 1860 Oxford evolution debate, Bishop Wilberforce is said to have asked his evolutionist opponent, Thomas Huxley,

WILBERFORCE: *You claim descent from a monkey; was this on your grandfather's or your grandmother's side?*

One response to a straw man is a concise statement of the real position:

HUXLEY (*poss.*): *Evolutionists do not claim that we are 'descended from monkeys'. We claim that apes, monkeys, and humans have common ancestors.*

A PERSONAL ATTACK (*argumentum ad hominem*) is also present, thinly veiled, in Wilberforce's statement. This nasty fallacy deliberately confuses someone's appearance, history or character with their argument (it is illogical to disagree with a person just because you don't like them). Huxley returned this curved ball in the manner befitting it:

HUXLEY: *I would sooner claim kinship with an ape than with a man who misuses his great gifts of oratory to stifle scientific debate.*

Appeals to the emotions have a long history of undermining logical reasoning and are widely used by politicians. Classic EMOTIONAL APPEALS such as the APPEAL TO FEAR, the APPEAL TO PRIDE, the APPEAL TO HATRED, the APPEAL TO JEALOUSY, the APPEAL TO PITY, the APPEAL TO COMMON CUSTOM, the APPEAL TO ANTIQUITY, the APPEAL TO MODERATION, and THE APPEAL TO SUPERSTITION are all used daily on the floors of parliaments and in the media:

DEVELOPER: *If we, the leaders of the world, don't build this new airport then our great nation will decline! Our luck will leave us. Our place will be taken by France. We and others before have always been brave. I beg you, do not walk away now!*

TESTING AN ARGUMENT
some useful techniques

When confronted with a complex argument, or trying to develop one yourself, it can be a good idea to test it. Here are three ways to do this:

1. **REDUCTIO AD ABSURDUM:** To falsify a hypothesis, begin by assuming that it is true. If, based on that assumption, you can prove a contradiction (an 'absurdity'), then you may conclude that your original hypothesis is false. Conversely, to prove a hypothesis is true, assume that it is false and see if absurdities result. Here is a time-proven example from Euclid:

> Let ABC be a triangle having the angle ABC equal to the angle ACB. I say that the side AB is also equal to the side AC. For, if AB is unequal to AC, one of them is greater. Let AB be greater; and from AB the greater let DB be cut off equal to AC the less; Let DC be joined. Then, since DB is equal to AC, and BC is common, the two sides DB, BC are equal to the two sides AC, CB respectively; and the angle DBC is equal to the angle ACB; therefore the base DC is equal to the base AB, and the triangle DBC will be equal to the triangle ACB, the less to the greater: which is absurd. Therefore AB is not unequal to AC; it is therefore equal to it.

2. **THE CONSEQUENTIA MIRABILIS** ('admirable consequence'): The *Consequentia*, like the *Reductio*, tests a hypothesis by initially assuming it is false. If, on the basis of that assumption, you are then able to prove your hypothesis, you may conclude that it is true.

38

Descartes' *Cogito, ergo sum* ('I think, therefore I exist'), paraphrased here, rests on a form of this logical move:

I am thinking. Granted that my thinking may be completely mistaken, I cannot deny that it is occurring. Applying the Consequentia, I assert: 'I am not thinking.' This cannot be true, as the statement 'I am not thinking' is itself the expression of a thought. Therefore I was right to assert that I was thinking.

3. OCCAM'S RAZOR: Abduction seeks a hypothetical cause which matches the known facts (*see p. 7*). When conducting such a risky undertaking, *Occam's Razor*, named after William of Ockham [c. 1287–1347], advises that a simple explanation is a better bet than a complex one. Newton gives the following 'philosophizing rule' at the beginning of the third part of the 1726 edition of *Principia*:

Rule I: We should not admit extra causes of natural events beyond such as are both true and sufficient to explain the phenomena in question.

Beware of OCCAM'S OVERDOSE. The true reasons for things are often very complex indeed, and bizarre concatenations of events do occur all the time, so use Occam with due caution.

AXIOMS
logical foundations

All logical systems ultimately rest on a set of *axioms*, statements which are unproven and unprovable (within the system) and taken to be self-evident. The process of proving further statements is then built on these. Traditional logic rests on three axioms, *The Laws of Thought*.

THE THREE TRADITIONAL LOGICAL AXIOMS:

1. THE PRINCIPLE OF IDENTITY. *A thing is itself.* 'I am myself'.

2. THE PRINCIPLE OF THE EXCLUDED MIDDLE. *Every statement is either true or false. It cannot be 'sort of' true. Through changing circumstances true statements may cease to be true, and false statements may become true, but in the end 'My cat is either alive or it's not'.*

3. THE PRINCIPLE OF NON-CONTRADICTION. *No statement can simultaneously be both true and false. 'It cannot be true and false that my cat is alive'.*

These axioms seem self-evident and commonsensical, but they do *not* hold true for every logical system. As we shall see in the following pages, Proposition 2 does not hold true for multi-valued logics (*see page 53*) and Proposition 3 does not hold true when we encounter a paradox (*see p. 42*). Both 2 and 3 also run into trouble in quantum theory, particularly if the cat belongs to Erwin Schrödinger [1887-1961].

A fourth law of thought formally joined the other three in the 18th and 19th centuries after a long journey, via Plato, Aristotle, Cicero, Avicenna, and Spinoza, though it too is vulnerable to paradox:

4. THE PRINCIPLE OF SUFFICIENT REASON. *Nothing exists, happens, or is true without a cause which can make it so (a 'sufficient cause'). Something cannot be self-caused, since it would logically have to precede itself.*

These axioms are by no means the only possible ones. For example, the four developed by Gottfried Leibniz [1646–1716] are similar to the traditional axioms, but also show intriguing differences.

LEIBNIZ'S FOUR FUNDAMENTAL AXIOMS:

1. THE PRINCIPLE OF IDENTITY $(A = A)$. *'I am myself'.*

2. *If (all) A is B and (all) B is C, then (all) A is C. So 'If all women are human beings', and 'all human beings are mortal', then 'all women are mortal'.*

3. *Something cannot be its own negation $(A \neq \text{not } A)$: So 'If I am mortal, I am not immortal (not non-mortal)'.*

4. *A positive statement of identity is equivalent to its reversed negation $(A = B$ is equivalent to (not B = not A). This is contraposition (see p. 23). So if 'I am a human being' then 'That which is not a human being is not me'.*

"Well, if you insist on using logic I see little point in continuing this argument."

PARADOX

this is a lie

All systems of logic complex enough to be generally useful sooner or later encounter *paradoxes*, instances where logic comes to an impasse like a machine with a spanner in its works. A paradox is an argument which has a *valid form and apparently true premises, but an apparently false or contradictory conclusion.* Perhaps the most vexing example is **THE LIAR PARADOX**, which has bedevilled logicians for at least 2500 years. Here it is in its most simple form:

> This sentence is false.

If this sentence is true, then it's false (that it's false). On the other hand if it's false, then it must be true. In either case it's a false assertion that it's false, so maybe it's true that it's false after all!

Perhaps the problem lies in the fact that the sentence refers to itself—maybe if we add a second line, the problem will go away:

> The following sentence is true.
> The preceding sentence is false.

But now the first sentence tells us to trust the second which tells us to distrust the first, so we should distrust the second, meaning we should trust the first after all. The logic is revolving endlessly around a contradiction, making it impossible to come to any conclusion. Maybe we should just ban words like 'sentence', but banning all metareferential statements would limit our ability to say things like 'This is a book is about logic'.

Metareferences are at the core of RUSSELL'S PARADOX, which was described by Bertrand Russell [1872–1970] in 1901:

> Let R be the set of all sets that are not members of themselves. If R is not a member of itself, then its definition dictates that it must contain itself, and if it contains itself, then it contradicts its own definition as the set of all sets that are not members of themselves.

Russell was trying to join mathematical logic to the real world, via the development of a perfect logical system. But in 1931 a young mathematician named Kurt Gödel presented a paper titled *On Formally Undecidable Propositions* which changed logic forever. It outlined his *Incompleteness Theorems*, which showed that any logical system more powerful than the most basic must have limits, and that in any axiomatic system (of mathematics or logic), there will always be at least one proposition which cannot be proven within the confines of that system. In the terminology of traditional logic this translates as

> In any system of logic, there will always be at least one statement which cannot be proved to be either true or false.

In other words, a paradox, with much in common with the self-referential Liar Paradox. In fact a 'Gödel question' may be formulated which will create a paradox in any logical system:

> In system L (for Logic), this statement is false.

If L stands for traditional logic, with its four axioms (*see p. 40*) then if the statement is indeed false according to L, then it is true that it is false. So it is true. Which means it must be false, and so on. Today logicians accept that the paradox is unavoidable and work around it.

THE SORITES
and other famous paradoxes

Paradoxes of parts and wholes form an interesting group. One example, discussed by Plutarch [c. 46–120 AD], is **THE SHIP OF THESEUS**:

> *Over many years Theseus repaired his ship. At a certain point, every piece of the ship had been replaced. It was still Theseus' ship, yet no material from the original ship remained. How can this be? And if someone built a ship out of all the discarded parts, which then would be the real Ship of Theseus?*

Or consider another example, known as the **SORITES PARADOX**, attributed to Eubulides of Miletus [4th century BC]:

> *There is a big heap of sand. Take one grain away and it's still a heap, as we agree that removing one grain of sand does not change a heap to a non-heap. Continue to remove one grain at a time, until there is a 'heap' of two grains, and then, removing one, a single grain of sand. This is clearly not a heap, but we agreed that removing a single grain does not change a heap to a non-heap.*

Thus we have a heap which is not a heap, violating the axioms both of identity and non-contradiction (*see page 40*).

These paradoxes seem to depend on the vagueness of natural languages. Perhaps there is some point at which a heap ceases to be a heap (or a ship ceases to be the same ship), but this point can't be specified. The same is true for anything which is a collection of smaller things: a crowd, say, or a multitude, or a plethora, or a human body, whose cells are always being replaced.

We could try to solve this paradox with multi-valued logic: maybe there is a size of sand-pile for which it is neither true nor false that it is a heap, or maybe everything is either a heap or not a heap, but it's not clear which is which. Maybe reality, like language, is fuzzy (*see p. 53*).

If you watch carefully, Eubulides uses fuzzy language to create some of his other famous paradoxes:

> **THE ELECTRA** paradox (*Elektra*) :
> *Electra doesn't know that the man approaching her is Orestes, her brother.*
> *Electra knows her brother. So does Electra know the man who is approaching?*

> **THE HORNS** (*keratinês*) paradox:
> *What you have not lost, you have. But you have not lost horns.*
> *Therefore you have horns.*

Zeno of Elea [490–430 BC] designed paradoxes around problems of time, space, and infinity:

> The **ACHILLES AND THE TORTOISE** paradox:
> *Achilles is racing a tortoise, which has a head start. He first must reach where the tortoise was, but by the time he gets there the tortoise has moved on, and when he gets to its new location, it has moved on again, etc. How can he ever overtake?*

Paradox is harnessed as a linguistic tool by many of the world's mystical traditions, to nudge students out of habitual ways of thinking and effect changes in their consciousness. The Zen *koan* is a classic example—a deeply paradoxical claim is made, and the student left to stew in the resulting lack of closure.

> *Two hands clap and there is a sound. What is the sound of one hand?* – Hakuin Ekaku

LOGICAL PROBLEMS
language and riddles

The human ability to reason with language has long been connected with the princely skills of problem-setting and problem-solving, and nowhere is this clearer than in so-called 'Logic problems'. Some of the earliest of these are riddles:

> *There is a house. One enters it blind and comes out seeing. What is it?*
>
> – Sumerian tablet, 1800BC.

> *Four hang, four sprang, two point the way, two to ward off dogs, one dangles after, always rather dirty. What am I?* – Icelandic *Hervarar Saga*, c.1250.

The successful solution of a riddle can require a particularly agile mind, and often the answer 'comes in a flash', while quite the opposite approach works for puzzles such as this one:

> *There are seven houses; In each house there are seven cats; Each cat catches seven mice; Each mouse would have eaten seven ears of corn; If sown, each ear of corn would have produced seven hekat of grain. How many things are mentioned in all?* – Rhind Papyrus, 1650 BC

This is in fact a mathematical question (and mathematics is intimately related to logic). Little imagination is required to solve it, unlike this medieval problem, related to the Liar paradox (*see p. 42*):

> *Before you are two doors. One leads to heaven and the other leads to hell. Before each door stands a guardian, one who always tells the truth, the other who always lies. You can ask one of them one question. What should it be?*

This can only be solved using pure logic, as can its tougher cousin:

There are three gods on an island. One always tells the truth, one always lies, and one answers randomly. The gods answer "da" or "ja" in their own language but you don't know which means "yes" and which means "no." You have three questions to work out which god is which. What should they be? – George Boolos, 1996

Or try this one, based on an original by Albert Einstein [1879–1955]:

There are five different colored houses, each with a man with a different nationality, favorite drink, food, and pet. The Englishman lives in the red house. The Swede keeps dogs. The Dane drinks tea. The green house is just to the left of the white one and its owner drinks coffee. The cabbage-eater keeps birds. The owner of the yellow house eats nuts while a man keeps horses next door. The man in the center house drinks milk. The Norwegian lives in the first house. The porridge-eater has a neighbor who keeps cats. The man who eats biscuits drinks beer. The German eats cheese. The Norwegian lives next to the blue house. The porridge-eater has a neighbor who drinks water. Who owns the fish? – after Albert Einstein

To solve problems like these logicians began to develop a special language of their own.

BOOLEAN ALGEBRA
and true or false

At the heart of logic is the quest for knowledge about the truth or
falsity of statements. Boolean algebra reduces truth and falsity to the
numbers 1 and 0, and replaces words like 'and', 'or', and 'not' with
operators, '∧', '∨', and '¬'. Logicians then convert statements into
notation and study their behavior using *truth tables*:

		AND	OR	
P	**Q**	**P∧Q**	**P∨Q**	*The truth table shows that 'if P is*
1	1	1	1	*true AND Q is true' is only true*
1	0	0	1	*when both P and Q are true. And*
0	1	0	1	*that 'If P is true OR Q is true' is*
0	0	0	0	*only false when P and Q are false.*

In Boolean algebra '1 and 1' = '1' (as there is no digit higher than 1);
and negation, '¬' or 'not', works by inverting a '1' into '0', or a '0' into '1'.

Boolean algebra mirrors many important
logical transforms. Try substituting 0 and 1
into the equations below:

DOUBLE NEGATION $P \Leftrightarrow \neg\neg P$
    "I'm fine" = "I'm not not fine"

TAUTOLOGY $P \wedge P \Leftrightarrow P$
    "I'm both well and I'm well" = "I'm well"
                  $P \vee P \Leftrightarrow P$
    "Either I'm cool or I'm cool" = "I'm cool"

48

Boolean algebra also allows you to flip logical statements just as you would mathematical equations:

COMMUTATION
$$P \wedge Q \Leftrightarrow Q \wedge P$$
"I'm fit and happy" = *"I'm happy and I'm fit"*
$$P \vee Q \Leftrightarrow Q \vee P$$
"I'm good or I'm bad" = *"I'm bad or I'm good"*

ASSOCIATION:
$$(P \wedge Q) \wedge R \Leftrightarrow P \wedge (Q \wedge R)$$
$$(P \vee Q) \vee R \Leftrightarrow P \vee (Q \vee R)$$

DISTRIBUTION:
$$P \wedge (Q \vee R) \Leftrightarrow (P \wedge Q) \vee (P \wedge R)$$
$$P \vee (Q \wedge R) \Leftrightarrow (P + Q) \wedge (P \vee R)$$

And finally, it allows you to rephrase logical arguments in interesting ways, with some interesting results (*as we shall see on page 50*).

MATERIAL IMPLICATION $\quad P \rightarrow Q \Leftrightarrow \neg P \vee Q$
"If there's a shootout, then you'll die" = *"There's no shootout, or you'll die"*.

TRANSPOSITION $\quad P \rightarrow Q \Leftrightarrow \neg Q \rightarrow \neg P$
"If I shoot, then you'll die" = *"If you haven't died, then I didn't shoot"*

IMPORTATION $\quad P \rightarrow (Q \rightarrow R) \Rightarrow (P \wedge Q) \rightarrow R$

DEMORGAN'S THEOREM $\quad \neg(P \wedge Q) \Leftrightarrow \neg P \vee \neg Q$
"It's false that I'm hot and angry" = *"Either I'm not hot, or I'm not angry"*
$$\neg(P \vee Q) \Leftrightarrow \neg P \wedge \neg Q$$
"I'm neither slow nor stupid" = *"I'm not slow and I'm not stupid"*

The entire modern electronic world rests on simple logical processes made possible by the basic Boolean algebra shown on these two pages.

PROPOSITIONAL LOGIC
how to build a robot

Propositional logic dates back to Chrysippus of Soli [c.279–c.206 BC], and the Stoics. Reinvented by Pierre Abelard [1079–1142] in the 12th century, it was later taken further by Leibniz, George Boole [1815–64], and Gottlob Frege [1848–1925], among others.

Propositional logic regards statements as its basic units and examines the ways they are linked by operators ('and', 'therefore', 'not', etc). It cannot address the truth of a classical syllogism based on the traditional rules of subject-predicate relation, but instead excels at manipulating and transforming complex arguments to probe their validity.

In addition, propositional logic does not recognise the nexus in conditional ('if') statements (*see p. 8*). So while in everyday logic, "*If the Earth moves around the sun, then dogs are mammals*" is false, since the two statements (despite both being true) are not connected by a valid nexus, in formal logic, "*If two plus two equals five* (F), *then summer is the warmest month* (T)" is true, as is "*If two plus two equals five* (F), *then all circles are square* (F)". These strange results come from the truth-functionality of transposition and material implication (*see previous page, and table below*).

p	q	FALSE (contradiction) ⊥	NOR (not or) ↓	Converse nonimplication ↚	Negation (not p) ¬p	Material nonimplication ↛	Negation (not q) ¬q	XOR (exclusive or) ⊕	NAND (not and) ↑	AND ∧	XNOR (exclusive nor) ⊙	Q projection q	Material implication →	P projection p	Converse implication ←	OR ∨	TRUE (tautology) ⊤
T	**T**	F	F	F	F	F	F	F	F	T	T	T	T	T	T	T	T
T	**F**	F	F	F	F	T	T	T	T	F	F	F	F	T	T	T	T
F	**T**	F	F	T	T	F	F	T	T	F	F	T	T	F	F	T	T
F	**F**	F	T	F	T	F	T	F	T	F	T	F	T	F	T	F	T

NAME	FORM	DESCRIPTION
Simplification	$p \wedge q \Rightarrow p$	p is true and q is true: therefore p is true
Conjunction	$p, q \Rightarrow (p \wedge q)$	p is true; q is true: therefore p and q are true
Addition	$p \Rightarrow (p \vee q)$	p is true: therefore p or q is true
Modus Ponens	$(p \rightarrow q) \wedge p \Rightarrow q$	If p then q; p: therefore q
Modus Tollens	$(p \rightarrow q) \wedge \neg q \Rightarrow \neg p$	If p then q; not q: therefore not p
Hypothetical Syllogism	$(p \rightarrow q) \wedge (q \rightarrow r) \Rightarrow p \rightarrow r$	If p then q, and if q then r; so if p then r
Disjunctive Syllogism	$(p \vee q) \wedge \neg p \Rightarrow q$	Either p or q, or both; not p: so q
Constructive Dilemma	$(p \rightarrow q) \wedge (r \rightarrow s) \wedge (p \vee r) \Rightarrow q \vee s$	If p then q, and if r then s; p or r: so q or s
Destructive Dilemma	$(p \rightarrow q) \wedge (r \rightarrow s) \wedge (\neg q \vee \neg s) \Rightarrow \neg p \vee \neg r$	If p then q, and if r then s; not q or not s: so not p or not r
Bidirectional Dilemma	$(p \rightarrow q) \wedge (r \rightarrow s) \wedge (p \vee \neg s) \Rightarrow q \vee \neg r$	If p then q, and if r then s; p or not s: so q or not r
Composition	$(p \rightarrow q) \wedge (p \rightarrow r) \Rightarrow p \rightarrow (q \wedge r)$	if p then q, and if p then r: so if p then q and r
Exportation	$(p \wedge q) \rightarrow r \Rightarrow p \rightarrow (q \rightarrow r)$	(if (p and q) then r) implies (if (q is true then r is, if p is)
Importation	$p \rightarrow (q \rightarrow r) \Rightarrow (p \wedge q) \rightarrow r$	(if q is true then r is, if p is) implies (if (p and q) then r)
Commutation (and)	$p \wedge q \Leftrightarrow q \wedge p$	(p and q) is the same as (q and p)
Commutation (or)	$p \vee q \Leftrightarrow q \vee p$	(p or q) is the same as (q or p)
Commutation (equal)	$p = q \Leftrightarrow q = p$	($p = q$) is the same as ($q = p$)
Association (and)	$p \wedge (q \wedge r) \Leftrightarrow (p \wedge q) \wedge r$	p and (q and r) is the same as (p and q) and r
Association (or)	$p \vee (q \vee r) \Leftrightarrow (p \vee q) \vee r$	p or (q or r) is the same as (p or q) or r
Distribution (and)	$p \wedge (q \vee r) \Leftrightarrow (p \wedge q) \vee (p \wedge r)$	p and (q or r) is the same as (p and q) or (p and r)
Distribution (or)	$p \vee (q \wedge r) \Leftrightarrow (p \vee q) \wedge (p \vee r)$	p or(q and r) is the same as (p or q) and (p or r)
Double Negation	$p \Leftrightarrow \neg\neg p$	p is the same as (not (not p))
Tautology (and)	$p \Leftrightarrow p \wedge p$	(p is true) is the same as (p is true and p is true)
Tautology (or)	$p \Leftrightarrow p \vee p$	(p is true) is the same as (p is true or p is true)
De Morgan (and)	$\neg(p \wedge q) \Leftrightarrow (\neg p \vee \neg q)$	not (p and q) is the same as not p or not q
De Morgan (or)	$\neg(p \vee q) \Leftrightarrow (\neg p \wedge \neg q)$	not (p or q) is the same as not p and not q
Transposition	$p \rightarrow q \Leftrightarrow \neg p \rightarrow \neg p$	(if p then q) is the same as (if not q then not p)
Material Implication	$p \rightarrow q \Leftrightarrow \neg p \vee q$	(if p then q) is the same as (not p or q)
Material Equivalence I	$p = q \Leftrightarrow (p \rightarrow q) \wedge (q \rightarrow p)$	($p = q$) is the same as ((if p then q) and (if q then p))
Material Equivalence II	$p = q \Leftrightarrow (p \wedge q) \vee (\neg p \wedge \neg q)$	($p = q$) is the same as ((p and q) or (not p and not q))
Material Equivalence III	$p = q \Leftrightarrow (p \vee \neg q) \wedge (\neg p \vee q)$	($p = q$) is the same as ((p or not q) or (not p or q))

Above: The elements of propositional logic, where arguments are formed from symbols and logical operators.

EXTENDED LOGICS
more like the world

In the real world things are rarely just true or false, so in the 20th century logicians like C. I. Lewis, Ruth Barcan, Lotfi Zadeh, and Saul Kripke extended predicate and propositional logic, making it more nuanced.

MODAL LOGIC applies qualifiers to logical statements. These qualifiers come in a number of different kinds:

ALETHIC: *measures certainty; 'possibly', 'contingently', 'necessarily true'* ...

DEONTIC: *considers ethical concepts; 'obligatory', 'ought', 'forbidden'* ...

EPISTEMIC: *deals with states of knowledge; 'it is known that' or 'unknown'* ...

DOXASTIC: *handles states of belief; x 'thinks that', 'will always think that'* ...

TEMPORAL: *qualifies in terms of time; 'was true', 'will be true'* ...

PROBABILISTIC: *deals with degrees of likelihood; 'probable', 'unlikely'* ...

Modal logics are useful for analyzing everyday philosophies with their embedded webs of possible/impossible, permissible/impermissible, and necessary/contingent concepts. Take the tricky future conditional:

If it rains tomorrow I shall stay at home!

Its truth value is impossible to determine before tomorrow comes, unless we admit modals like 'probable'. Other arguments, like the *Ontological Argument for the Existence of God* (see p. 55), rely on the modals 'possible' and 'necessary/must'. Modal logic can also treat ethical or aesthetic questions which lie outside the purview of traditional logic:

Mary believes that if you are beautiful you ought to be generous and kind

But there's not enough space to display the algebra for that here.

FUZZY LOGIC deals with grey areas of truth, using a (sometimes infinite) number of values between true and false; e.g. from a survey:

Very true [ ]   Mostly true [ ]   Partially true [ ]   Not at all true [ ]

Fuzzy logic is useful in the real and messy world, and allows logicians to work with to statisticians, risk analysts, and others.

QUANTUM LOGIC permits qubits to exist in a superposition of 1 and 0 (truth and falsity) until the system is observed. *Shor's algorithm* allows quantum computers to discover the answer to difficult questions without having to calculate—they simply freeze at the right answer. Mathematical physicist Roger Penrose has suggested our brains may likewise operate as quantum systems, explaining human intuition.

The mysterious relationship between reality and the language we use to describe it is at the core of the logical process (*see also p. 43*):

'There's glory for you!'
'I don't know what you mean by "glory",' Alice said.
Humpty Dumpty smiled contemptuously. 'Of course you don't — till I tell you.'
'When I use a word,' Humpty Dumpty said, in rather a scornful tone, 'it means just what I choose it to mean — neither more nor less.'

– Lewis Carroll, Through the Looking Glass

Human infants acquire language fast and often ask 'why?' as soon as they can talk, thus both engaging in inductive reasoning (causes and effects) and associating words with things. Considering this mystery, the German philosopher Ludwig Wittgenstein [1889–1951] eventually concluded:

Whereof one cannot speak, thereof one must remain silent.

GOOD AND TRUE
logic and ethics

Logic is good at assessing statements of fact, but things get more tricky with modal statements involving words like 'ought' or 'should'. In particular, ETHICAL DILEMMAS ask you to consider how you should behave in a particular situation, and can reveal the way your rationality interacts with your character and your priorities:

> LIFEBOAT DILEMMA: *Your ferry has sunk in the middle of the ocean and you and five other adults are crammed into a tiny lifeboat which is leaking badly. With everyone bailing water the lifeboat can just stay afloat. A second lifeboat, in better condition, comes over and a friend who you met on the ferry invites you to join them, as there is room for one more. What should you do?*

Situations like this occur extremely infrequently in most people's lives, but they are the staple diet of scriptwriters and moviegoers.

> BOMBER DILEMMA: *An old psychiatric patient of yours has planted huge bombs all over a large town. If they go off thousands of people will die. He has been caught but is refusing to disclose the bomb locations unless you hand over your six-year-old daughter. You remember he has a intense terror of torture. The clock is ticking. What should you do?*

Dilemmas like these cleverly exploit the fact that, as Aristotle realised 2500 years ago, our natural human capacity for reason is not purely logical. In the same way that rhetoric can decorate a logical argument, everyday instincts, such as self-preservation, loyalty to friends and family, and social codes of behavior, can play havoc with our logical faculty when we try and figure "what should I do?".

To help put goodness on a more logical foundation, 18th and 19th century ethical systems attempted to quantify the good:

Act only according to that maxim whereby you can, at the same time, will that it should become a universal law. – Immanuel Kant, 1785

Always act to maximise happiness for the most number. – John Stuart Mill, 1861

By and large, these maxims have become axiomatic to much modern ethical reasoning, seemingly even enabling 'the greatest good' in many difficult situations to be analyzed and calculated.

Logical systems are circumscribed; they can deal with matters under their purview, but they cannot 'see' outside their parameters. It has been argued by many thinkers, beginning with Plato, that certain issues of great importance—the Good, the True, and the Beautiful— lie ultimately beyond the ability of human thought and language to comprehend. It may be that logic can prove to us truths about the highest realities (*as in the modal Ontological Argument, below*), but it cannot show us these realities in their entirety.

1. *It is possible that a supreme being exists.*
2. *In other words, a supreme being exists in some possible world.*
3. *But if it really is supreme, then it must also exist in every possible world.*
4. *And, if it exists in every possible world, then it must exist in the actual world.*
∴ *A supreme being exists.*

Indeed, the master logicians of the past indicate an understanding which ultimately transcends logic. From Aristotle to Boole, key thinkers have erected their systems as ladders to be kicked away once successfully climbed. Hopefully, you too have now reached this stage, and can now enjoy the full practice of dialectic, the search for Truth.

APPENDIX - LIST OF FALLACIES

FORMAL FALLACIES

FALLACIES OF THE SYLLOGISM:

AFFIRMATIVE CONCLUSION FROM A NEGATIVE PREMISE (*p. 18*): Can occur when one or more premise is negative.

EXCLUSIVE PREMISES (*p. 18*): Two negative premises generate no necessary conclusion.

EXISTENTIAL FALLACY (*p. 19*): Arguing from a *universal* (All X / No X) to an *existential* (therefore X exists) (not everyone thinks this is fallacious).

ILLICIT TREATMENT OF THE MAJOR OR MINOR TERM (*p. 19*): Treating a term as distributed in the conclusion which is undistributed in the premises.

NEGATIVE CONCLUSION FROM AFFIRMATIVE PREMISES (*p. 19*): Can occur when all premises are affirmative.

QUATERNIO TERMINORUM, 'Four terms', (*p. 18*): A syllogism must have precisely three terms in order to be valid.

UNDISTRIBUTED MIDDLE TERM (*p. 15*): Where the middle term is not universal ('all') in at least one premise.

OTHER FORMAL FALLACIES:

AFFIRMING A DISJUNCT: Assuming in a disjunctive (P or Q is true) argument, that affirming one of the options implies the falsity of the other.

AFFIRMING THE CONSEQUENT (*p. 21*): Assuming in a conditional (if P then Q) sentence, that because the consequent (Q) is true, the antecedent (P) must be too.

FALLACY FALLACY: The mistaken assumption that just because a logical argument contains a fallacy that its conclusion must be wrong.

FALSE CHOICE (Imperfect Disjunction or *Bifurcatio*), (*p. 27 & p. 35*): A disjunctive (either/or) premise must state the only possibilities; if another exists, the disjunction is false

CONCLUSION WHICH DENIES PREMISES (*p. 5*): In traditional logic no conclusion can deny its own premises.

CONFUSING SUBSTANCE AND ACCIDENT (*p. 13*): Whe qualities of things are treated as things in their ow right, substance and accident have been confused.

CONJUNCTION FALLACY: The mistaken assumption th the probability of multiple conditions occurring w be higher than for any of the single conditions alone.

CONTRADICTORY PREMISES: Premises which contradict eac other imply anything (the 'principle of explosion').

DENYING THE ANTECEDENT (*p. 22*): Assuming in conditional (if P then Q) sentence, that because th antecedent (P) is false, the consequent (Q) must be to

MASKED MAN: Denying identity based on relative subjective properties: "I know my father; I do n know that masked man; therefore, that masked ma is not my father".

NECESSITY: Imputing unwarranted necessity. "All bachelo are unmarried; John is a bachelor; so John canne marry". In fact John's marital status *can* change!

INFORMAL FALLACIES

AESTHETIC FALLACY: The use of beauty in debate, e.g., mathematics, "this is just too beautiful to be false".

ANALOGICAL FALLACY: The use of an analogy which lac relevance and evidence. "It's good to grow your ow food" "Really? You sound like Chairman Mao". (*p. 34*)

ANECDOTAL FALLACY: The use of an anecdote, sometimes vivid one to distract from the argument. "Skiing kee you so fit" "Yeah? My first husband died skiing!"

ANTIQUITATEM, argumentum ad: 'Appeal to antiquity'. "I ancient, tested by time!" Inverse of *ad novitatem*.

ASSOCIATION FALLACY: Just because two things sha some property does not make them alike in oth ways. "Blue is Conservative; The sky is blue; The s is Conservative"

CULUM, argumentum ad: 'Appeal to the rod'. Replacing argument and reasoned refutation with the threat of physical harm, discomfort, blackmail, etc. A crude form of avoiding the issue, *Ignoratio Elenchi*.

COMPLETE EVIDENCE or 'Cherry Picking'. The biased selection of data to support a position while suppressing contradictory evidence.

RCULUS IN PROBANDO: Circular Reasoning (*p.34*).

MPOSITIO: 'Placing together', a.k.a. Composition (*p.30*). One is an odd number. Two is made up of two ones. Therefore two is an odd number. Inverse of *Divisio*.

ONSEQUENTUM: The fallacious use of the desirability or undesirability of an argument's outcomes. "If P then Q will happen, and we don't like Q, P must be false".

ONTINUUM: The fallacy of the beard, sorites, etc. Wrongly rejecting a claim because it is not precise. Human language often blurs boundaries, but such vagueness does not automatically create invalidity.

RUMENAM, argumentum ad: 'The appeal to wealth'. Assuming someone's wealth is an indicator of possession of the truth. Inverse of *ad Lazarum*.

UM HOC ERGO PROPTER HOC: 'With this, therefore because of this'. Assumes that two or more events which occur together are causally linked, simply because they occur together (*p.5 & p.33*). Should not be pushed too far; often, co-occurrence *is* evidence of a causal link.

EFECTIVE INDUCTION: The inductive fallacy, or 'Jumping to Conclusions' or 'Hasty Generalization' (*see p.32*). "1, 3, 5 and 7 are prime; 9 is square; 11 and 13 are prime. So all odd numbers are either square or prime."

CTO SIMPLICITER: A fallacy of accident in which exceptions are taken to invalidate rules. "I saw a cat with three legs, therefore cats cannot be defined as four-legged animals". *Reverse of Compositio*.

VISIO: Division (*see p.30*). The English love cricket. Tom is an Englishman. Therefore Tom loves cricket. Inverse of *Compositio*.

ONKEY FALLACY: Those bad guys are attacking an argument, so it must be good and true.

QUIVOCATIO: Equivocation. The fallacy of using the same word or words in two or more distinct significations in a single argument (*p.31*).

FRAMING FALLACY: a.k.a. 'Loaded Question'. Posing a question in a misleading way to give a bad conclusion.

HOMINEM, argumentum ad: 'Argument against the man'. The Personal Attack (*p.37*). The use of an opponent's appearance, character or background to discredit them. A form of *Ignoratio Elenchi*.

INVIDIAM, argumentum ad: 'The appeal to jealousy'. A form of emotional appeal (*p.37*).

IGNORANTIUM, argumentum ad: 'The appeal to ignorance'. The fact that something has not been disproved does not make it true.

IGNORATIO ELENCHI: 'Ignorance of the argument'. Various forms include *The Red Herring*, *Avoiding the issue*, the *Straw Man* and the *Irrelevant Thesis/Conclusion*. Someone seems to be proving or refuting something, but is actually doing something else (*pp.36-37*).

INFINITUM, argumentum ad (also *nauseam*): Wearing down an opponent through repetition of an argument.

LAPIDEM, argumentum ad: 'Appeal to the stone'. Dismissing an argument as ridiculous with no proof. Samuel Johnson, when asked about Bishop Berkeley's argument that only mental objects really exist, said 'I refute it thus!' and kicked a stone.

LAZARUM, argumentum ad: 'The appeal to the poor' (the biblical Lazarus having been a poor man). The fallacy that poor, simple people are less subject to corruption or vice than the vicious rich. Inverse of *ad Crumenam*.

METUM, argumentum ad: 'The appeal to fear'. An *Emotional Appeal* (*p.37*). "If you X you will die".

MISERICORDIAM, argumentum ad: 'The appeal to pity'. "I deserve a better grade; my mother is sick".

MODUM, argumentum ad: 'The appeal to moderation' or false compromise. "You say it's spelled with an A; I say it's Z; so the correct answer is probably around M."

NATURALISTIC FALLACY, 'is-ought': Occurs when someone argues for what *ought* to be the case on the basis of statements about what *is* the case.

NO TRUE SCOTSMAN: Reinforcement of a blunt assertion.

DAD: "No Scotsman puts sugar on his porridge". KID: "But uncle Angus puts sugar on his". DAD: "Ah yes, but no *true* Scotsman puts sugar on his porridge!"

Non causa pro causa: ' non-cause in place of a cause'. The informal fallacy of False Cause (*p.33*).

Non sequitur: 'It does not follow'. A general term for any invalid inference, where the conclusion is not entailed by the premises.

Novitatem, argumentum ad: 'Appeal to the new'. "It's newer, so it's better!" Inverse of *ad antiquitatem*.

Odium, argumentum ad: 'The appeal to hatred'. "Prisoners should dig roads because prisons are full of scumbags!"

Onus Probandi: Shifting the burden of proof (*p.35*). "Prove me wrong, otherwise I'm right".

Overwhelming exception: Asserting something as an exception to a rule, when it falsifies the rule. "We are a loving peaceful people, except when we are at war."

Petitio principii: Also known as "Begging the Question" (*p.34*). Giving an argument's conclusion as a premise.

Plurium interrogationum: 'Of too many questions'. A fallacy which smuggles several questions into a single one, and then demands a simple answer (*p.33*). A specialised form of *petitio principi*.

Populum, argumentum ad: 'The appeal to the populace'. An emotional appeal which maintains that, if lots of people do/say/believe it, then it must be true (*p.37*).

Post hoc ergo propter hoc: 'After this, therefore because of this'. The false assumption that because an event followed another event, there must be a causal link between them (*p.33*). Closely related to *Cum Hoc Ergo Propter Hoc*.

Red Herring: Trying to divert an argument by changing the subject. "Why did you hit your sister?!" "Mum, the neighbor's dog is in our garden again" (*p.36*).

Relative Privation: The invalid introduction of an extreme comparison. "Well, it's not as bad as X".

Secundum Quid, a.k.a. 'Destroying the Exception': An informal fallacy of accident where exceptions to a rule are ignored and the rule applied to all cases with no exceptions (*p.32*).

Sentimens superior: Any emotional appeal which seeks show that feeling is superior to rational thought.

Shift of Imposition/Intention, fallacy of: These fallacie arise from the erroneous use of a term (*p.11*).

Silentio, argumentum e: 'Argument from silence'. Sayir that lack of evidence constitutes evidence.

Slippery Slope Fallacy: Occurs when it is claime that choosing a particular course of action will sta something on a slippery slope to somewhere wors i.e. when a minor action will cause a major impa through a long chain of loosely logical relationships.

Straw Man Fallacy: Covertly replacing an argument wi a false proposition (the "straw man") and then easi defeating that weaker argument (*p.36*).

Superbiam, argumentum ad: 'The appeal to pride.' Th use of flattery in an argument. A form of emotion appeal (*p.37*). "You look great in that car, so buy it!"

Superstitionem, argumentum ad: 'The appeal t superstition'. A form of emotional appeal (*p.37*).

Temperantiam, argumentum ad: *see Modum*.

Texas Sharpshooter Fallacy: Ignoring differences i data while stressing similarities. Its name comes fror a story about a 'gunman' who repeatedly fires at a bar door, and then paints a target on the largest cluster.

Tu quoque: An *ad hominem* fallacy invoking hypocritic behavior in an opponent relating to the conclusior "How can you argue X when you're doing Y?"

Two wrongs: Don't make a right. "You stole a banan from Sue!" "I know, but Sue stole it from Eric!"

Vacuous Truth Fallacy: The use of empty sets in a argument. E.g. saying "I ate up all the turnip on m plate" to Mum when Nanny didn't feed you any turnip

Verbosium, argumentum: 'Wordy argument'. The us of excessive and obfuscatory verbiage to hide th weakness of an argument.

Verecundiam, argumentum ad: 'The appeal to shame A proposition is claimed to be true simply becaus a respected figure says it is true. The shame enter when the opponent accepts this false authority (*p.37*)

ERRATUM: *There is a false statement on page 58.*